Ready

Ready for Marriage?

Nicky & Sila Lee

Alpha International
London

ISBN 10: 1 905887 02 7
ISBN 13: 978 1 905887 02 6

Published by Alpha International
Holy Trinity Brompton
Brompton Road
London SW7 1JA

Email: publications@alpha.org

Ready for Marriage?

How do we know that we are right for each other? What happens if we are not compatible? Is it normal to have doubts? Do we have a realistic view of married life?

When we are contemplating marriage, these may well be some of the questions that we are asking ourselves. Such questions must be faced honestly.

In this booklet we list seven tests of love which are designed to reveal whether we have the foundations upon which to build a strong marriage.[i] These tests help to show not only if we are right for each other but also if we are ready for marriage.

Marriage must be based on more than infatuation.

Feelings of 'in loveness' will not sustain a marriage for a lifetime. Infatuation wears off, but these following seven aspects of love can grow stronger over the years.

TEST 1: Do I want to share the rest of my life with this person?

Marriage is about two individual people, who have been leading individual lives, coming together and sharing everything. Does the thought of doing so fill me with excitement or uncertainty?

Marriage does not allow us to remain as two independent people living in the same house, using the same bed and spending a lot more time together. Marriage means being ready to share our whole lives with another person.

Am I ready to share my time? I have been used to organising my own agenda in my own way. Now we will need to work out our agenda together. Marriage does not mean spending every minute together, but it does mean always taking each other into account when we make our plans.

Am I ready to share my money? Could I honestly say, *'Whatever is mine will become ours'*? In marriage there is nothing that remains mine alone, for we promise in the wedding vows that *'all my worldly goods with you I share.'* Every possession I have, large or small, valuable or sentimental, is to be shared with another person. Am I ready for that?

TEST 2: Does our love give me energy and strength or does it drain me?

If the relationship is healthy, we shall feel more alive when we are together and more motivated to live to our full potential. The other person's love should set us free to be the person we were created to be.

Marriage (contrary to many people's perception) can be liberating. The experience of a strong marriage is of living a life that is renewed by another's love.

Does being together make each of us more rather than less of a person?

Our closest friends or family are often the people who recognise most accurately the effect of the relationship on us. If we bring out the best in one another, other people want to be around us. Does being together make each of us more rather than less of a person?

This second test reveals whether our love motivates and inspires us. For some couples, the sheer effort involved in keeping the relationship going drains them and causes them to feel trapped. That is not a healthy basis for marriage. They may have been going out with their partner for some time and are afraid of hurting them by breaking off the relationship. But it is better to break up sooner rather than later if the relationship has no long term future.

TEST 3: Do I respect this person?

There will be different aspects that attracted us to each other. Respect, however, goes deeper than mere attraction.

Do I respect this person's character? We discover

someone's character by seeing the way they relate to others: how they treat older people, younger people, their family, their peers, those from a different background, culture or race. Do they show compassion, courage, perseverance, patience, consistency and any other qualities we value highly? They may be stunningly good looking, have a high powered job, be a brilliant cook or an outstanding athlete, but are they kind? (If in doubt, watch the way they treat their mother.)

Do I respect their judgment? What about the decisions they make, big or little, about career, money or family?

Are we compatible in our core beliefs and values? It would be unwise to marry someone with strongly opposing views on those things we hold most dear.

"If we had a bet on the 2.45 at Ascot – we could double our honeymoon budget"

For example, do we agree on matters of faith, ethical issues, education, children? To find out that our partner does not want children can be a very painful discovery with implications for the rest of our life.

If you are a Christian, the Bible's injunction not to *'be yoked with an unbeliever'* (2 Corinthians 6:14) is important advice for those considering marriage. Does this person want to follow and serve God wholeheartedly in every aspect of their life? Does he or she look to God as the one who has a plan and purpose for their life (and therefore for your life together)?

Can I say to myself, 'I would be proud to be attached to this person'? A telling question to ask is, 'Would I like this person to be the mother or father of my child?'

TEST 4: Do I accept this person as they are?

None of us is perfect. We all have our weaknesses, quirks and bad habits. What annoys us about this person?

We need to be sure that we could live together and love each other even if none of these things were to change. We must not get married on the instalment plan, hoping to change this or that about our partner once married. We will usually be disappointed.

We must not get married... hoping to change this or that about our partner

Addictive behaviour, such as with alcohol, drugs, gambling or pornography, will often require professional help and should be addressed prior to marriage, because getting married won't in itself solve these addictions. (See the information for contacting a counsellor at the back of this booklet.)

TEST 5: Are we able to admit our mistakes, apologise and forgive one another?

Conflicting ideas and negative feelings are an inevitable part of any close relationship. Paul Tournier in his book *Marriage Difficulties* states,

'Disagreements are entirely normal. As a matter of fact, they are a good thing. Those who make a success of their marriage are those who tackle their problems together and who overcome them.' [ii]

When we hurt one another, we need to be able to bring it out into the open... say sorry and forgive.

When we hurt one another, we need to be able to bring it out into the open, let go of our pride, say sorry and forgive. This requires good communication. Have we as a couple settled disagreements between us in a constructive way?

The point of this test is not the existence or absence of conflict but our ability to resolve it.

TEST 6: Do we have interests in common as a foundation for friendship?

Do we have fun together? Friendships are built on shared experiences. Shared activities lead to shared confidences and shared memories. Have we found interests that we both enjoy? Do we derive pleasure from doing things together? Marriage does not involve sharing every interest but it will be important to continue with these and other joint activities once married to keep our friendship growing.

TEST 7: Have we weathered all the seasons and a variety of situations together?

Have we seen each other through a summer and a winter – in shorts as well as in an overcoat? Or have we only seen each other with washed hair and ready to go out? Do we know the whole person? Have we known each other not only when things are going well but also when times are difficult? How do we each respond when unwell or under stress or in a crisis?

> Have we known each other not only when things are going well but also when times are difficult?

Some people rush into marriage because they have been hurt by a previous relationship or a tragedy in their life. Getting married as an escape from pain is an insecure foundation for any relationship. Only sufficient time together will reveal the real person. As someone has said, *'Love is what you've been through with somebody.'*

Some people can answer yes to all seven tests, yet struggle to make the commitment of marriage because in their past someone they trusted let them down. Their parents' marriage may have been abusive; their father or mother may have left the family home when they were at an impressionable age; they may have suffered through the breakdown of a previous relationship that they had hoped would last for life.

The first step in overcoming a fear of commitment is to recognise its source. Talking about it with a trusted friend, church leader or counsellor helps. (It is generally better to discuss doubts about our relationship with someone other than our partner.)

The second step is to forgive those who have hurt us (If this is a parent, use the prayer in Chapter 15 of *The Marriage Book* as a basis.) When forgiveness is an on-going process each time the pain, anger or disappointment resurfaces, gradually the memories have less and less hold on us. For many, however, their fear of commitment is ultimately resolved through knowing the faithfulness of their partner, through growing in trust, and through experiencing at first hand a loving marriage.

We have happily married friends who could have answered yes to all seven tests, but on their wedding day were still wrestling with hesitation and doubts. It takes courage to tie the knot and to say words that will affect the rest of our lives.

We know others who have been brave enough to break off an engagement within a few weeks or even days of their wedding. Some have subsequently got married to someone else; others have remained single. They have not regretted their decision.

Better by far to be single and independent, using our freedom to serve God and to reach our full potential in him, developing many friendships along the way, than to suffer the consequences of an ill-chosen husband or wife.

> It takes courage to tie the knot and to say words that will affect the rest of our lives.

If you make the decision to go ahead or are already engaged, we recommend you prepare for your marriage by doing *The Marriage Preparation Course*, which is now being run in many different locations.

Engagement, with all the busyness of organising a wedding, can feel like entering a whirlwind of planning and activity. The course provides the opportunity to focus on your marriage and to build strong foundations for the future. While based on Christian principles, the five sessions are very practical and are suitable for any engaged couple, whether or not they are Christians themselves. Some couples who are not engaged do the course as a way of exploring further what is involved in getting married.

Marriages must constantly be nurtured and so we also run *The Marriage Course*, which we recommend couples attend two years or so into their marriage.

For more information:

Please see our websites: www.marriageprepcourse.org and www.themarriagecourse.org.

For counselling information: www.acc-uk.org

Recommended reading

Rules of Engagement by Katharine and Richard Hill
Look Before You Leap by J.John
The Marriage Book by Nicky and Sila Lee
The Mystery of Marriage by Mike Mason
The Sixty Minute Marriage by Rob Parsons

Notes

[i] These tests have been adapted from *I Married You* by
Walter Trobisch (IVP 1971) pp. 89-92.

[ii] Paul Tournier, *Marriage Difficulties* (SCM Press 1971)
p. 26.